NEW LIGHT ON CULTS

Therese M Donnelly

Precinct Press

NEW LIGHT ON CULTS

First edition. January, 2019.

Imprint: Independently published under the Precinct Press label.

ISBN: 9781793996619

CONTENTS

Introduction   1

Examples of Religious Cults   3

How to Recognise a Contemporary Cult   8

Why People Join and Stay in Cults   15

Why Reject Established Religions?   24

What Motivates Cult Leaders?   27

Cult Use of Traditional Religious Teachings   30

Leaving a Cult   36

Concluding Thoughts   41

Quotations About Religious Cults   44

The Author's Cult Experience   46

Bibliography   48

About the Author   49

Reviews   50

Works by the Same Author   51

INTRODUCTION

The Concise Oxford Dictionary defines a cult as "a system of religious worship; devotion, homage to a person or thing."

Though not all contemporary cults could be described as religious, the one thing such groups have in common is that *they address people's needs.*

Some groups are overtly religious, others offer a method of self-improvement such as doing yoga exercises to improve health, or they teach ways to act more effectively in daily life. Anyone can be attracted to such a group without realising that behind the scenes lurks something sinister.

People join a group of like-minded people drawn together in an attempt to have their needs met - they don't knowingly join a cult.

Most self-improvement groups are benign but given the scandals that occur periodically, it's clear a minority are not. In the public mind, unsurprisingly, the word "cult" is most likely associated with something undesirable: scandals over a cult leader's sex life, religious distortion, kidnapping, bizarre teachings, murder, and mass suicide.

This book, written from personal experience, explores both the negative aspects and positive benefits of cult life, with a particular emphasis on how personal needs are met within a cultic group.

EXAMPLES OF RELIGIOUS CULTS

Clearly, not all contemporary religious cults or other types of cult, though they may be damaging in some ways, end as catastrophically as some of those existing in the 1990's. That decade was notable for the number of cults that ended in disaster for their followers.

1. 1993 saw the deaths by fire and shooting of members of the Branch Davidians in Waco, Texas. The Branch Davidians had their origins in a breakaway group of the Seventh Day Adventist Church in 1929. David Koresh, who joined the group as a handyman in 1981, became their leader in the mid-1980s. A major recruitment drive in 1985 attracted followers from around the world and 130 men, women and children lived at the Waco compound by the time of the 51 day siege and final conflagration in 1993.

2. 1994, 1995 and 1997 revealed deaths by fire and shooting of members of the Order of the Solar Temple in Switzerland, France and Canada. Founded in 1977 by Luc Jouret, a homoeopathic physician, he convinced his followers that he had been a member of the Knights

Templar, a Catholic military order, during the time of the Crusades.

Followers, who believed Jouret to be the Messiah, were recruited through public lectures which he gave in Switzerland and Canada. In October 1994 48 bodies, some of them dressed in ceremonial robes, were found at two sites in Switzerland. All had been subject to burning, murder or suicide. In France 16 people were found having been shot dead. Much later, five other followers were found dead near Montreal, Canada, three with stab wounds.

3. 1995 brought deaths and injuries on the Tokyo subway in a nerve gas attack by the Aum Shin Rikyo sect. Aum Shin Rikyo was led by a blind Japanese guru who reputedly heard a voice telling him to "lead God's army".

In 1986 Shoko Asahara created a left-wing communal society at the foot of Mount Fuji, which a year later was recognised as a religious institution by the Japanese government. The group's membership grew rapidly reaching more than 25,000 by 1988.

Like David Koresh, and later Marshall Applewhite of the Heaven's Gate sect, Shoko Asahara's teaching focused on an approaching apocalyptic war from which Asahara would emerge to lead Japan and possibly the world. In 1995 the group released nerve gas on the Tokyo subway killing twelve people and injured 5,000, apparently as part of an attack on the country's constitution and civil institutions.

4. <u>1995</u> saw the sexual scandals of the Nine O'clock Service (NOS). The NOS was a religious group led by the Rev. Chris Brain, based at an Anglican church in Sheffield, England between 1988-1995. The group combined preaching with rock music, dancing and stunning visual affects to attract and influence a youthful congregation. The leader reputedly grew to live a life of luxury and sexual excess at his followers' expense.

5. <u>1997</u> revealed mass suicide in a San Diego suburb by members of the Heaven's Gate sect. The sect was started in the 1970s by Marshall Applewhite and Bonnie Nettles, a nurse he met whilst a patient in a psychiatric hospital. They convinced themselves that their mission was to prepare the way for the Kingdom of Heaven.

Applewhite and Nettles travelled through the USA attracting followers through public lectures. After Bonnie Nettles died of cancer, Applewhite continued to lead the group until the mass suicide in 1997. Applewhite and his followers imagined they were leaving planet earth to join a spaceship believed to be travelling behind Comet Hale Bopp. Autopsies revealed that several followers, including Applewhite, had been castrated.

Pre-dating these disasters by many years, is that most infamous of tragedies known as the Jonestown Massacre. In Guyana, in 1978, 914 Peoples' Temple followers of the cult leader Jim Jones killed themselves.

Following the murder of US Democratic Congressman Leo J. Ryan, and three news reporters, plus injuries to others, Jones directed his followers to poison themselves and their children, which they did, against a backdrop of desperate screaming.

Despite these disasters new religious groups continue to be a worldwide phenomenon. Most go unreported but a few of the more extreme attract media attention.

Cult members from a Christian sect known as the Church of Almighty God were reported being arrested recently in China, for killing a woman who wouldn't join their group; the Islamic Faizrakhmanist cult in Russia was raided and followers found in squalid conditions living underground; and Nxivm, a self-help group based in Albany, New York, had women in the inner circle branded with a two inch square symbol as part of their initiation, according to a report in The New York Times.

In 2018, A South Korean cult leader, Pastor Lee Jaerock, described as a 'God' by his followers was jailed for 15 years following his conviction for raping eight of his female supporters.

In case the reader is tempted to rush to judgement about the mentality of cult members, it is important to recognise that no-one knowingly joins a destructive cult. As W. M. Grossman wrote, "These situations develop step by step; no-one, if asked says "Oh yes. I'd like to join a cult and burn to death in a siege" any more than anyone intentionally chooses the life of a battered wife or a drug addict."

It is true to say however, that in the most extreme cults, some followers do eventually lose all powers of reasoning.

HOW TO RECOGNISE A CONTEMPORARY CULT

W hy is it when people are attracted to an organised group of like-minded people, they are unaware they may be joining a cult?

Cults can take many forms, and when a potential member makes their first contact with a cultic organisation, they may meet with only a small group of the cult's members, and not see the bigger picture.

Making it more difficult to identify them, cults can take forms other than those with a religious or spiritual slant, such as self-improvement and psychotherapy groups, and political and commercial organisations. Some cults mix ideas, as in Aum Shin Rikyo, which had both a religious and a political agenda.

Some cults originate from the established religions, for example, Christian groups with a focus on dramatic healing claims or the casting out of devils.

Others, such as Scientology, form around an innovative system constructed by the leader. Yet others combine traditional teachings with new ideas. Aum Shin Rikyo, for example, had its roots in Buddhist-Taoist-Hindu traditions. The Branch Davidians took their ideas from the Old and New Testaments as did the Heaven's Gate sect. The Order of the Solar Temple had its origins in the Knights Templar of the Crusades.

Several cults have arisen as off-shoots of the twentieth century fourth way teaching of George Gurdjieff and his best known pupil, Peter Ouspensky - teachings which are geared towards spiritual evolution.

So, aside from the different types of cults which serve to confuse the picture, another difficulty is that contemporary cults are organizations in a condition of gradual and constant change, and an enthusiast may encounter a group in its early, middle or late stages of evolution. Furthermore, cults tend to be secretive.

At its beginning, a cult may consist of a small group of people focused around a charismatic leader to whom individuals are attracted, and from whom they can receive the sort of guidance they've been seeking. As the group grows it becomes more organized until at its end, it can become a manipulative, exploitative, multi-national organization.

What most people mean when they speak of a cult, is a group which has acquired the characteristics of *mid-late stage evolution*. They are unaware of the initial form of the cult and what attracted early joiners to it. Some cults, however, such as the Heaven's Gate sect, failed to attract large numbers perhaps because from the beginning, their extreme ideas were too radical for most potential recruits to accept.

It is possible, by drawing an imaginary evolutionary line, to identify the point on the line to which a group has evolved, and to anticipate how the group might be expected to develop in the future.

Though researchers have identified approximately forty characteristics of cults, it is only necessary to *observe the lifestyle of the leader and the attitude of followers to the leader*, to make a diagnosis of a group that has evolved into the damaging stages of its existence, and should be avoided at all costs.

This writer, having experienced fourteen years of cult life and who has studied the histories of several contemporary cults, has established that they evolve in a similar way. Listed below are twenty stages of cult evolution. **Note however**, that not all cults will pass through each stage and stages will overlap:

<u>Early Stage</u>

1. People encounter an attractive, small group within which a charismatic leader has emerged or is self-appointed.

2. The leader's followers are enthused by the ideas being taught and begin to focus on the group to the exclusion of other people and activities in their lives.

3. The followers are asked to make financial contributions to support the leader and group activities, and they are willing to do so.

4. The group enlarges and enthusiastic members form

emotional bonds, united by common aims and activities.

During this first stage, some of the needs of the members are met and there are no obvious downsides, aside from a minor financial burden for some.

<u>Middle stage</u>

5. The attention and adulation of the followers gradually elevates the leader above his or her peers.

6. The leader begins to change. Flattered, but drained by the constant attention and demands of the followers, the leader's view of their self becomes distorted. Bolstered by the growing conviction of their God-like status, the leader may consider there is no earthly authority to which he or she is answerable. The leader makes claims to be the sole guardian of the truth.

7. The group continues to grow to the point where formal organization becomes necessary. Dedicated followers, especially the wealthy, are rewarded with positions of responsibility.

8. Demands for financial contributions increase and become burdensome for many.

9. The group adopts a missionary role and expands its presence including into other countries.

10. The group may apply for charitable status. It runs businesses, and by now, the annual financial turnover of the group may be substantial.

11. The group is highly structured with several people in positions of power over others. The leader may be unaware of the way his or her subordinates exercise their power.

During this middle stage, the follower may still find benefits in membership but the danger signs are growing.

Late stage

12. Should followers show signs of doubting the leader and the direction the group is taking, fear of the consequences of leaving is instilled in them in order to convince them to stay.

13. The leader begins to live away from the main body of the group, often in luxurious conditions, in contrast to those experienced by the members.

14. People desiring power and control gravitate towards the leader and form a clique around him or her.

15. The clique protects the leader in order to protect its own interests. The leader is now out of control, testing his or her autocratic powers to their limits. The power clique, who by now may have lost respect for the leader, nevertheless attempt to prevent followers from recognizing the deterioration in the leader, in order to protect their own interests.

16. News of the leader's shortcomings begins to leak out to the wider membership. The press begin to show an interest in the group's activities. The leadership

comes under attack both from outside and within the group.

17. Law suits are served by the organization against those publicly critical of it. Former members challenge the group with law suits. Where possible, the cult reaches out of court settlements.

18. While some dissident members may be expelled, other followers are held fast in the grip of the cult, some against their will.

19. The leader and power clique resort to increasingly extreme and desperate measures in order to maintain their position and silence opposition. Financial demands increase, telephones may be tapped and even arms purchased.

20. At its most extreme, a catastrophic denouément ensues - public scandal, attempted murder, murder, imprisonment, and suicide.

The collapse may be followed by the emergence of a re-formed group from amongst the surviving members.

All the above are danger signs, which if spotted by a prospective member, should tell them to steer well clear.

All along the evolutionary line of development, people join and leave the organization. During their time in the group members may be at its heart, in the middle, or out on the fringes. Their position within the organisation will demonstrate the depth of their involvement, and how easy or difficult it is for them to leave, should they consider doing so. People on the fringes i.e. those living far from the group's headquarters, are largely immune to, or unaware of, the situation at the centre.

In summary, by the time a religious cult has evolved to its late stage, the leader is authoritarian, declaring herself or himself to be divine and is considered so by many followers. In a non-religious cult, the leader is slavishly followed. Following the leader, is believed to be the only route to enlightenment, salvation or other ultimate aim - as defined by the cult. The leader lives in luxurious circumstances at the followers' expense, removed from the main body of the group. The leader is largely inaccessible except to a privileged few. Lawsuits fly and unfavourable press reports appear. The leader makes prophecies of future events which the group prepares to encounter. Prophecies fail, yet because *they need to,* followers continue to manifest unquestioning submission to the leader, treating him or her like a celebrity or saint.

Despite the publicized tragedies that have occurred and some of the nonsense that goes on in these groups, they continue to proliferate and flourish.

It's time to look at what people hope to gain by joining such a group.

WHY PEOPLE JOIN
AND STAY IN CULTS

People join cults for several reasons but what is *most significant is that they join to have their needs met.* These needs may be recognized by the individual but it's more likely they're not.

A common feeling on meeting a sympathetic group is that "this is exactly right" or "this is what I have been looking for" and feeling no doubt about that. This is true of any special interest group but meeting a religious cult can be an especially emotional moment.

Subconsciously, the individual senses that a lot, if not most of their needs, can be met within the group. The impact of the teachings and the welcoming energy of the group can be such that interest in being anywhere else or doing anything else ceases. At last, what has been so desperately sought has been found and the more unmet needs a person has, the more powerful the attraction and adherence to the group.

The following is a summary of cult members' needs and what lies behind them:

The Need to Satisfy a Deep Spiritual Longing

A longing for spiritual knowledge and understanding of the purpose and meaning of life may have lasted many years and nothing has yet been able to satisfy it. Many books will have been read on a range of spiritual ideas and several spiritual development methods may have been tried but none has yet provided answers that satisfy the seeker.

Is this need met? This depends on what the cult leader is teaching, what system of ideas they are using, how the ideas are presented and the depth and breadth of the teaching. If the cult leader answers some of the questions the seeker has previously been unable to answer for themselves, there will be a desire to stay and learn more. Other members who have already been convinced by the leader, will repeat and reinforce the cult leader's teaching.

The Need for Self-improvement and Self-esteem
Most people feel a need to improve themselves. When they make comparisons between themselves and others they can feel inadequate.

Is this need met? Many cults provide members with opportunities to learn new skills e.g. food preparation, cooking meals for large numbers, waiting at tables, horticulture and gardening, raising livestock, vehicle mechanics, craft work, teaching, and organising meetings and social events. There may be opportunities to learn about fine wines, music, literature and art. All of these activities are provided as part of the work of the cult, usually at no additional cost to the membership, though there is usually a financial cost involved in being a member of a cult, often a heavy one.

The Need for Self-knowledge and Understanding
It is difficult for a person to know themselves well. Most people can see other people's strengths and weakness but cannot see themselves as others see them.

Understanding is different from knowledge. It is feasible to know something about one's self but not understand what lies behind it. You might, for example, know that you prefer going to bed late, or noticed that you always seem to be in dispute with someone or other, or that you start things with great enthusiasm but can never finish them.

Is the need met? Many people feel a need to understand why they are the way they are and want to know more about themselves, and a cult leader will often comment on an individual's behaviour and encourage other members to do so in order to bring actions into awareness. However, the observations offered can be difficult to accept and demoralising if not delivered with compassion.

The Desire to Make a Difference in Life
There is a need in most people to have an impact on life, to be able to change things for the better. The reality however, is that few are able to achieve much of any significance on their own, either locally, nationally or globally, and most feel that what efforts they do make are limited in their effects.

Is this need met? One of the benefits of cult life is that

the cult usually has a clearly defined purpose which members can identify with, such as survival of the cult following a nuclear holocaust and the re-building of civilisation. Thus, the cult provides a sense of being able to bring about positive change on a grand scale. The reality is, however, that cults rarely have an impact beyond their own boundaries and the prophecies of impending doom, fortunately for all, remain unfulfilled.

The Need for an Aim, Purpose and Meaning
Most people need clear aims in order to focus their energy. They also need to feel that there is a real purpose to their efforts.

Is this need met? In a religious cult, the leader suggests not only short and long-term aims for the individual so that they can develop, but also major objectives for the group, usually related to the survival of a forthcoming natural or man-made catastrophe. Personal survival, being a primary instinct, is a major motivation for staying within the group.

Many people experience a sense of meaningless about life at some time, especially when faced with the death of relatives and close friends, and meaninglessness can be disabling if it is persistent. Suicide is known to occupy the minds of many in their pre-cult days. Membership of a cult can counteract this depressed state of mind by providing meaning, direction, and purpose to its members lives.

The Longing for a Better Way of Life

Many who join cults have led unsatisfying lives up until the point they join. Dissatisfaction with inappropriate housing, a dull job, a stifling family life, and poor close personal relationships can all contribute to a cult member's openness to the new opportunities offered.

The Need for Guidance and a Structured Way of Life

A cult provides a distinct structure for an individual's life, whereas previously, they may have led a life of doubt, insecurity and an unfocused use of time.

Is this need met? In a cult there is a timetable of events for the day or week including regular meetings and mealtimes. This structure provides a secure framework within which to develop through involvement in these activities. Members are encouraged to develop beyond their imagined limitations by accepting the challenge of unfamiliar work, and by working with others, or subordinate to them, and all for an inspiring aim.

Many people feel lost in the chaos of life and don't know what to do with themselves. They feel there is no-one they can ask for help, at least no-one they have confidence in, so they welcome having a leader to tell them what to do. In a cult, the system of work and the leader, provide an aim and direction for a follower's life.

There are downsides however. People can be become too dependent on others directing their lives such that they fail to mature and take responsibility for themselves. They can also be taken advantage of, by being expected to work for extremely long hours for little or no physical reward, in pursuit of the cult leader's aims.

The Desire for a Sense of Self Worth

The aims of a cult can provide an individual with a heightened sense of their own personal value. Members, at least initially, become happier, younger looking, cleaner, tidier and more productive. The tasks of the cult can provide a member with a sense that their contribution, not just within the cult, but also to humanity, has real significance.

Because of the cult's teachings, members feel chosen from the mainstream of life and may consider their group to be superior to other similar groups and religions. Being part of cult life makes people feel special. This can breed an unrealistic and unjustified sense of superiority over others.

The Need to be of Service in Ways which are Meaningful to Them

There are many opportunities to be of service in life such as work within churches and charities. But cult members feel their own needs need to be addressed before they can give their time and energy to others.

Is this need met? People become involved in activities which have meaning for them, and for some, the spiritual dimension and development opportunities that are provided in cults, are what is most significant. It could be said that charitable work would provide ample opportunity for personal development, which is true, but charitable work fails to satisfy other needs which potential cult members have.

The Need to Feel Optimistic

Cult membership offers an individual hope for the future. Whereas previously they may have suffered many setbacks in life and become disillusioned by the world around them, the cult provides the hope of achieving spiritual or other aims, at the same time as making a significant contribution to the future of humanity.

The Need to be Loved and Appreciated

At first, cult members welcome newcomers and accept them regardless of their age or background. Meeting a cult can be a very emotional time for those who have been deprived of positive support.

The Need to Meet New People

A cult provides the opportunity for meeting many people and therefore there are new relationship possibilities. Previously, there may have been limited opportunities to find a partner or a reluctance to venture out to meet people.

Is this need met? Whereas prior to the cult experience, people may have felt lonely and isolated, cult members are rarely alone. Even though individual members may differ from one another greatly in terms of age, education and occupation, the experiences of group membership create strong emotional bonds through companionship and a shared purpose.

On the flip-side a cult can be a competitive environment where members seek to out-do each other in terms of spiritual and physical effort, and where people vie for the attention and approval of the cult leader.

The Need for Power, Control and Influence

When contemplating Armageddon or other such catastrophes, preparations being made by the cult give the impression that through working together they would survive and flourish, whereas outside the group, members would be powerless and at the mercy of events. There may be the idea that if the right personal sacrifices are made, destructive events will work out in a member's favour.

Is the need for power and control met? Because in the normal course of life an individual can feel overlooked and their worth unacknowledged, in the cult there is usually a hierarchical structure so members can see opportunities to gain power and influence. In particular, the idea of being a self-realised being, leading and teaching others and being admired and respected by many, is an attractive and motivating prospect.

Other Needs

Other reasons for joining a cult can be as simple as wanting to give up smoking, or find a partner, and the novelty value of cult membership can't be overlooked. Being part of a secretive organisation can be alluring to some since there exists an attraction in discovering and being part of what is hidden from others.

Those especially needy for attention will enjoy altering their appearance, dressing differently, adopting a new and unusual name and taking part in exotic rituals and ceremonies. By doing so, they enjoy appearing unusual and special.

These wide-ranging needs suggest compelling reasons why people are attracted to new cultic groups, and the reasons why they stay. It is not only, as is often suggested, that followers are brainwashed; it is just as likely they are held hostage by their own needs.

WHY REJECT ESTABLISHED RELIGIONS?

Why, if spiritual longing and needs are so strong, do people who join religious cults reject established religions? The answers may lie with their rejection of the demand for *belief* found in established religions.

Part of spiritual longing is the wish to find answers to important questions such as: who or what is God; why am I here; what is the purpose of existence; if "God" is good why is there so much suffering in the world; and what happens when I die?

The seeker's peers appear content with a predominantly materialistic lifestyle and appear relatively untroubled by such questions. Whereas, for some prospective cult members, there is a deep and insistent longing for answers and the established religions fail to provide answers that satisfy the enquirer.

Too often, what some established religions expect of their members is belief in unconvincing credal statements. Potential cult members are often too intelligent to accept religious statements without question. They demand more than that. Ironically, cults also require belief.

Established religions tell their members what they should do, but they don't explain how, and the question 'why' is answered by statements that require belief: 'Because God said such-and-such' or, 'In the bible it says such-and-such', therefore it must be true.

Firstly, no-one has yet defined exactly what is meant by 'God', nor has anyone proved that 'God' even exists. Secondly, since the Bible has been subject to many translations and interpretations over centuries, how can anyone be certain that what is stated is accurate?

Yet there persists for some people (and reasonably so), a keen sense that behind the facade of everyday life, something hidden, mysterious and spiritual does indeed exist and awaits discovery.

In a cult, particularly in its early stages when member numbers are low, there exists a greater possibility of personal guidance from the group leader. Intelligent questioning is encouraged for which the leader can suggest answers not found elsewhere. The leader may even teach an innovative system of development offering new knowledge leading to deep understanding.

Religious cults can provide a forum for questioning and exploration; a journey inwards to the essence of the self to find a place of knowing and understanding. On this journey, with the right knowledge and effort, illusions are shed, emotional wounds healed and verifications preferred to belief. Followers can question the notion of God, explore many levels of meaning and embrace a wider view of their self.

Established religions on the other hand, impose practices and behavioural restraints, and expect belief without understanding. They place boundaries on a person's thinking, demand the observance of ritual, and gain obedience by generating fear of the consequences if resolve weakens.

Established religions invite potential followers to a life of constriction and limitation rather than exploration and discovery. People are told they must love because it is the thing to do, and 'God' said so, rather than because they have journeyed within to love's source, enabling them to act from understanding.

Regrettably and perhaps inevitably, even contemporary, harmless cults, which in their early stages promise so much to the follower, once they become dogmatic and ritualistic, become indistinguishable from the established religions.

WHAT MOTIVATES CULT LEADERS?

I f deep-seated needs help to attract and retain cult members, what motivates contemporary cult leaders?

1. A Passionate Interest in a Body of Significant Ideas

The leader is enthusiastic about a body of ideas that have been a great help to them and which they feel they have a duty to pass on to others. Furthermore, they want to be able to teach and lead others in their own way, without constraints.

2. Imitation

The leader may have been part of a group and decided they have learnt enough to teach others and are keen to adopt the same appealing lifestyle their teacher had. This is all very well, provided they are not exaggerating their understanding and ability. A give-away is their frequent reference to other's teachings, such as the Bible. They make use of others to fill in the gaps in their own first-hand experience. When no new ideas or insights are offered to a group, it suggests the leader's understanding and development have stalled due to lack of personal efforts.

3. A Longing for Power and Recognition

They want the admiration and respect of followers and to become a big 'somebody', unaware they risk being tripped up by their own vanity – vanity being a well-known major obstacle to an individual's evolution.

4. A Desire to Avoid Personal Difficulties

They want to be supported financially by others so they never have to get a job and work for others again. Furthermore, they may like the idea of having followers they can use as servants to take care of all the essential, mundane tasks of life in which they have no interest.

Three further points about cult leadership motivation are worth consideration:

1. Inadequate recognition during childhood can result in a lifelong craving to make good this deficiency.

2. Should the group leader be single for whatever reason, not being married would not be questioned in the group since recognised spiritual leaders in the past (and some in the present) have been unmarried. If intimate relationships have been difficult, cult leadership can be a way to avoid the committed relationship issue, and provide same-sex or opposite-sex opportunities that might not otherwise be available.

3. For a few, group leadership represents a promising business opportunity.

4. The leader may have many unrecognised needs *identical to the needs of followers.*

As it happens, leaders don't get an easy ride. Leadership can lead to isolation and loneliness. Leaders become drained and exhausted by the insatiable demand for attention by dependent followers.

Followers place the leader on a pedestal, admiring their good qualities and rationalizing their deficiencies. What the leader says is often distorted, misunderstood, and needs to be corrected.

Under constant pressure from followers, hungry for their time and attention, it is scarcely surprising that leaders run the risk of losing their sense of direction and disconnecting from reality. This assumes their intentions, when starting the group, were honourable.

A leader may begin to lead their group motivated by sincere convictions and then go astray. Or they may have come to a realisation of their own deficiencies but press on, unable to admit to them, thereby damaging not only their own evolution by living a life of deceit, but also misleading their followers. On the other hand, from the beginning, a cult leader may have acted deliberately, with craft and cleverness, deceiving others for their own ends.

CULT USE OF TRADITIONAL RELIGIOUS TEACHINGS

Besides fulfilling needs, a group exercises a strong hold on followers through the religious element in the leader's teachings.

Most people are introduced to religious ideas from a young age when, because of their openness and vulnerability, the ideas penetrate deeply. Thus, the use of traditional religious ideas in contemporary cults, touches an irresistible chord in many and renders members more controllable.

The following are quotations from Judeo-Christian scriptures, specifically St Matthew's gospel, that a cult leader might use to influence and control the behaviour of their followers, and justify their own actions.

The cult leader suggests the followers have been chosen from the mass of humanity and are therefore special:

<u>Matthew 7.6.</u> Give not that which is holy unto the dogs, neither cast ye your pearls before swine, lest they tram-

ple them under their feet, and turn again and rend you.
Matthew 13.10-11. And the disciples came, and said
unto him, Why speakest thou unto them in parables?
He answered and said unto them, "Because it is given
unto you to know the mysteries of the kingdom of
heaven, but to them it is not given."
Matthew 13.16. But blessed are your eyes, for they see;
and your ears, for they hear.
Matthew 22.14. For many are called, but few are
chosen.

**The cult leader instructs the followers to be prepared
to sacrifice everything for spiritual development**:

Matthew 4.18-20. And Jesus, walking by the sea of Gali-
lee, saw two brethren, Simon called Peter, and Andrew
his brother, casting a net into the sea: for they were
fishers. And he saith unto them, "Follow me, and I will
make you fishers of men." And they straightway left
their nets, and followed him.
Matthew 6.31-33. Therefore take no thought, saying,
What shall we eat? or, What shall we drink? or, Where-
withal shall we be clothed? (For after all these things
do the Gentiles seek;) for your heavenly Father kno-
weth that ye have need of all these things. But seek ye
first the kingdom of God, and his righteousness; and all
these things shall be added unto you.

**The cult leader tells the followers to ignore warnings
from outsiders that they may be making a mistake**:

Matthew 5.11-12. Blessed are ye, when men revile you,
and persecute you, and shall say all manner of evil

against you falsely, for my sake. Rejoice, and be exceeding glad: for great is your reward in heaven: for so men persecuted they the prophets which were before you.

The cult member must learn to endure suffering and humiliation:

<u>Matthew 7.14.</u> Because strait is the gate, and narrow is the way, which leadeth unto life, and few there be that find it.

<u>Matthew 10.38.</u> And he that taketh not this cross, and followeth after me, is not worthy of me.

The follower must be willing to make efforts and sacrifices:

<u>Matthew 16.24-26.</u> Then said Jesus unto his disciples, "If any man will come after me, let him deny himself, and take up his cross, and follow me. For whosoever will save his life shall lose it: and whosoever will lose his life for my sake shall find it. For what is a man profited, if he shall gain the whole world, and lose his own soul? or, what shall a man give in exchange for his soul?"

The cult leader encourages followers to relinquish attachments to family and friends:

<u>Matthew 4.18-20.</u> And Jesus, walking by the sea of Galilee, saw two brethren, Simon called Peter, and Andrew his brother, casting a net into the sea: for they were fishers. And he saith unto them, "Follow me, and I will make you fishers of men." And they straightway left their nets, and followed him.

Matthew 8.21-22. And another of his disciples said unto him, "Lord, suffer me first to go and bury my father." But Jesus said unto him, "Follow me; and let the dead bury their dead."

Matthew 10.34-37. Think not that I am come to send peace on earth: I came not to send peace, but a sword. For I am come to set a man at a variance against his father, and the daughter against her mother, and the daughter-in-law against her mother-in-law. And a man's foes shall be they of his own household. He that loveth father or mother more than me is not worthy of me: and he that loveth son or daughter more than me is not worthy of me.

The cult member is encouraged to imagine that by following the cult leader they can become a more powerful person:

Matthew 17.19-20. Then came the disciples to Jesus apart, and said."Why could not we cast him out (a devil from a sick child)?" And Jesus said unto them, "Because of your unbelief: for verily I say unto you, if ye have faith as a grain of mustard seed, ye shall say unto this mountain, remove hence to yonder place; and it shall remove; and nothing shall be impossible unto you."

The cult needs its members to give what they have to the group and accept a life with few possessions:

Matthew 20.21-24. Jesus said unto him, "If thou wilt be perfect, go and sell that thou hast, and give to the poor, and thou shalt have treasure in heaven: and come and follow me." But when the young man heard that saying, he went away sorrowful: for he had great possessions. Then said Jesus unto his disciples, "Verily I say unto you, that a rich man shall hardly enter into the kingdom of heaven. And again I say unto you, it is easier for a camel to go through the eye of a needle, than for a rich man to enter into the kingdom of God."

The follower is enticed by the possibility of receiving special powers once they reach the inner circle of the group:

Mark 16.15-18. And he said unto them, "Go ye into all the world, and preach the gospel to every creature. He that believeth and is baptized shall be saved; but he that believeth not shall be damned. And these signs shall follow them that believe; in my name shall they cast out devils; they shall speak with new tongues. They shall take up serpents; and if they drink any deadly thing, it shall not hurt them; they shall lay hands on the sick, and they shall recover."Matthew 13.10-11. And the disciples came, and said unto him, "Why speakest thou unto them in parables?" He answered and said unto them, "Because it is given unto you to know the mysteries of the kingdom of heaven, but to them it is not given."

The cult discourages its members from requiring proof of the leader's validity:

Matthew 16.1-4. The Pharisees also with the Sadducees came, and tempting desired him that he would shew them a sign from heaven. He answered and said unto them, "When it is evening, ye say, it will be fair weather: for the sky is red. And in the morning, it will be foul weather to day: for the sky is red and lowering. O ye hypocrites, ye can discern the face of the sky; but can ye not discern the signs of the times? A wicked and adulterous generation seeketh after a sign; and there shall no sign be given unto it, but the sign of the prophet Jonas." And he left them, and departed.

The cult encourages a childlike dependency on the leader:

Matthew 18.2-4. And Jesus called a little child unto him, and set him in the midst of them. And said, "Verily I say unto you, except ye be converted and become as little children, ye shall not enter into the kingdom of heaven. Whosoever therefore shall humble himself as this little child, the same is greatest in the kingdom of heaven."

(Quotations are taken from the authorized King James' version of the New Testament published by Collins Clear-Type Press)

LEAVING A CULT

There are different ways of leaving a cult and each brings its own difficulties. If the attachment is strong, being forced out through failing to make financial payments is especially hard. Being expelled for rebelliousness, less so, since the cult member is already dissatisfied.

Extracting people from cults against their will is undesirable unless there is a plan in place to meet the follower's needs *in a way that feels right for them* – not to please other people, or do what other people think the follower *should* be doing.

Leaving a cult through choice is not easy unless the follower has been a member for only a short time. If the follower has been a member for several years there are many challenges to address. However, once a person does feel the urge to leave, it means they are ready to face the consequences of their action. They have identified at least some of their needs, and ways to meet them, as they prepare to move on with their life.

Those who leave of their own accord do so for various reasons. Work on inner development may have matured them to the point where remaining in the cult is no longer appropriate. Others leave because their needs are no longer being met and disillusionment has set in, or more is expected of them than they are willing to give. For example:

1. Someone with a longing for power and control is not given the position of responsibility they feel they merit.

2. A person hungry for attention fails to receive the recognition they feel they deserve.

3. There is a lack of satisfactory answers to questions, which tempts the follower to look elsewhere.

4. They are excluded from the power clique at the centre of the group so the leader is inaccessible to them. This results in jealousy and disappointment accompanied by the sense that they are losing out, because the presumed enlightened personal guidance of the leader is unavailable to them.

5. For some, the commitment and financial payments become too burdensome. Debts mount and the future begins to look bleak especially for an older person with few financial resources. And there is doubt as time goes on, that the group will provide the support they are likely to need.

6. Remaining ceases to feel appropriate for the individual's further development. They may lose interest and want to return to their old lifestyle. Personal life changes such as bereavement, marriage or parenthood can alter their perspective. Or, the experience gained and growing maturity, mean that the follower no longer has the needs that motivated them when they

joined.

7. A few recognise the falseness of the leader and the deterioration in the group, and are fortunate to have the means and strength to walk away.

Often it is hard to leave, not only because the cult's teaching on the subject of leaving has instilled the follower with fear of the consequences of doing so, but because the follower is held hostage by their own needs. For this reason alone, some stay even when they begin to have an idea that all is not well, because the group has become the only place which meets their deepest needs, hopes and dreams.

Others remain, unwilling to relinquish friendships or leave family members behind in the group. Yet others stay through fear of the challenges that await in the outside world – getting a job, finding somewhere to live, and making new friends.

A further deterrent to leaving is the matter of the time, energy and money that has been invested in membership and the sense of waste that the prospect of leaving brings.

Followers are right to be cautious about leaving because it can be disturbing and disorientating to walk away from friends, community, a structured life, purpose and aspirations, when membership of a group has lasted many years. And embarrassment at some of the idiotic ideas subscribed to also has to be faced.

THE POST-CULT
EXPERIENCE

The post-cult experience encountered by former followers is variable because it depends on the type of cult and the place the individual occupied within the organisation: close to the heart, somewhere in the middle, or living at an out-lying centre, where they may have been largely unaware of the more extreme aspects of the group. It also depends on:

1. How long they were members.

2. The strength of their commitment to the group and its teachings.

3. Whether they left of their own accord, were banished or 'rescued'.

4. Whether they were abused emotionally, physically or sexually.

5. Whether they left alone or with others. Those who walk away at the same time as others, have an advantage over those who don't, since they have the support and understanding of fellow leavers.

Whatever the cause or motivation, leaving is an uncomfortable experience requiring significant adjustment in thinking and behaviour.

The task of adjustment for former long-term members can be monumental. They may need to re-establish contact with their family and make new friends though they feel they have little in common with non-group members. Finances probably need attention, a career has to be resurrected, and a new home found. A new way of living must be established along with a sense of purpose and hopes for the future. Some join other groups, some start their own, others are left disillusioned.

The readjustment can last many years as the more extreme ideas of the cult begin to lose their grip. Part of the readjustment process consists in reviewing what was learnt, and reaching an understanding of the reasons for having joined.

It is also important for the former member to review the group's teachings and decide which ideas should be retained because of their usefulness, and which abandoned as unhelpful or no longer appropriate.

CONCLUDING THOUGHTS

I t would be best if anyone considering joining a new religious or other self-development group, would first attempt an honest appraisal of their personal needs. Then, explore ways in which their needs could be met that are self-empowering, rather than subjecting themselves to the power and control of others. For some however, especially those with strong spiritual longings who reject traditional religions, even if they are aware of their many needs, it could be that no better alternative to a new religious group presents itself.

Most people will never need to be concerned about the risk of joining a cultic group and even if they do unwittingly join one, their intelligence, common sense, and conscience will prevent them from coming to harm. Being educated about the dangers would help all to stay safe, particularly those more vulnerable and easily impressed.

For those with strong spiritual longings, looking for meaning in their lives, there are benefits in new religious group membership:

1. Companionship with like-minded individuals.

2. A shared interest and purpose.

3. Members become happier.

4. The group is often satisfyingly productive and efficient.

5. New opportunities and experiences are available, such as travel and learning new skills.

6. The follower is encouraged to develop beyond their imagined limitations.

7. They gain in confidence.

8. And above all, there is a chance to fulfill an aim to focus on an exploration of the spiritual aspects of life.

The downside, however, is the competitiveness of the environment, financial difficulties, inappropriate dominance by the leader and other members, emotional and physical abuse, and the real risk of sexual coercion in some form.

There is also the grave risk that in being pushed beyond natural inclinations (which, when done correctly encourages personal growth), followers gradually bury their consciences and act in ways that lead to wretched consequences for themselves and others.

When joining a new religious or cultic group, new members don't always appreciate that it's not meant to be a lifetime experience, contrary to what a group leader may tell them. As one former member wrote, "schools (in this case referring to Gurdjieff groups) are places for learning not retirement."

At some point a follower, however committed they were at the beginning, will most likely leave. This is the moment when they will realise how unwise it was to have abandoned old friends or neglected their family. They may regret not keeping a home and job and the amount of money they have given away. In a reasonable group under legitimate leadership, none of these sacrifices would be expected of a follower. They are not essential for self-development or spiritual evolution.

One of the major difficulties, is that once a follower leaves a group, their support network disappears. Also, they're no longer surrounded by others who remind them of the need for continual efforts in order to evolve – if that remains their aim.

Since other followers act as reminders to work, inevitably on leaving personal efforts slacken. It is important, therefore, that a leaver remain in touch with former members if possible, in order to keep their aspirations alive, and for the support such networking provides.

Finally, how much better it would be if anyone considering joining a self-development, cultic or new religious group would do so prepared to learn, share with others as they learn, pay if necessary, make efforts, *but always with an eye to leaving when they sense the time is right.*

QUOTATIONS ABOUT RELIGIOUS CULTS

"People who end up in cults are normal people. They are usually intelligent, open-minded and honest. They're willing to make sacrifices for the greater good of the group. They're interested in self-improvement and in the improvement of the world. The best kinds of people, in a way, are targeted by cults. Their very decency makes them desirable as cult members." *Dr J W West, Professor of Psychiatry, University of California.*

"These situations develop step by step; no-one, if asked says "Oh yes. I'd like to join a cult and burn to death in a seige" any more than anyone intentionally chooses the life of a battered wife or a drug addict." *W M Grossman.*

"Are we simply prejudiced against new religions? After all Christianity was small once too, and lots of people have died for it over the centuries." *W M Grossman.*

"I know that fasting, silence, solitude, sleep deprivation, and other techniques have long been used by different religious traditions. I believe they can be very useful and liberating in terms of unfreezing one's own habitual conditioning. They become unethical and destructive when they are used in combination with deception and a diminution of personal choice and integrity." *S Hassan.*

"Unselfishness, kindness, gentleness and compassion should be a basic living principle, not just an ideal. When individuals claim to be spiritually more developed, and put themselves in the role of guru, swami, master, prophet, these virtues must be consistently demonstrated." *S Hassan.*

"It is never appropriate for teachers, therapists or spiritual masters to take advantage of a power differential over followers. This is especially true in the area of sexuality. It is grossly unethical to engage in sexual relations with someone who has placed their trust in a teacher/advisor/master." *S Hassan.*

"Leaving alone is really, really hard. It felt, to me, like I had gotten a divorce from a thousand people and retained custody of nothing." *A.C.*

THE AUTHOR'S CULT EXPERIENCE

T he author was introduced to the 'fourth way' teaching of George Gurdjieff at an early age, having been lent a copy of Peter Ouspensky's book "In Search of the Miraculous." Though excited by the ideas in the book, longing to join a Gurdjieff group was not satisfied until ten years later.

Though the group joined was inspired by the teachings of Gurdjieff, a lot of what he had taught was missing. However, key teaching on the practical methods of self-development was clearly communicated and the organisation provided ideal circumstances for inner work.

There followed fourteen years of consistent efforts and enthusiastic membership at an out-lying centre of the organisation. Then, maturity and a growing sense that the group was deteriorating, and alarm bells sounding about the behaviour of the leader, resulted in walking away.

Though Gurdjieff groups consider themselves different from cults and some call themselves "schools", they may evolve into cults and bad things can happen in them. However, many people who join such groups derive great benefit, especially in the early years of membership. This writer's experience and the following quotations from former Gurdjieff group members confirm this:

" ..... the (cult) was the biggest and most unusual event to happen to us."

" ..... the most intensely concentrated educational experience of my life."

" .....the (cult) experience was special despite all the baggage that came with it."

" ..... a time of accelerated learning. I would not change a hair of it."

BIBLIOGRAPHY

Annett, Stephen. The many ways of being. Abacus 1976.

Barrett, David V. Sects, cults and alternative religions. Blandford 1996.

Grossman, Wendy. Cults: on the borderline and beyond. i to i, July-Sept 1993.

Harrison, Shirley. Cults: the battle for God. Christopher Helm, London 1990.

Hassan, Steven and Lama Surya Das. Avoiding abuses and pitfalls along the path. James Thurber 1995.

Houman, Peter and Andrew Hogg. Secret Cult. Lion Publishing 1984.

Ryder, Elizabeth. Preying on your mind. Nursing Times v.89 no.19 May 1993.

ABOUT THE AUTHOR

Therese M Donnelly is a non-fiction writer who enjoys writing about a wide range of subjects. Her primary passion is spiritual development.

If you've enjoyed reading this book or received value from it in any way, please consider leaving a review on Amazon. Thanks kindly!

For convenience, the QRCodes on the following page will take you directly to the "New Light On Cults" book page.

REVIEWS

Use your Smartphone to scan the following QR codes to leave your book review.

amazon.co.uk

amazon.com

OTHER WORKS BY THE AUTHOR

Cameras & Photography
Guide to the 1980's Disc Camera

Genealogy
My Life & Family History

Writing & Literature
Shakespeare Selected Quotations

The above books are available from all amazon websites worldwide.

Made in the USA
Monee, IL
01 September 2021

77076314R00032